RATTLESNAKE ALLEGORY

RATTLESNAKE
ALLEGORY

poems

Joe Jiménez

Red Hen Press | *Pasadena, CA*

Book design by Mark E. Cull

Library of Congress Cataloging-in-Publication Data
Names: Jiménez, Joe, author.
Title: Rattlesnake allegory : poems / Joe Jiménez.
Description: First edition. | Pasadena, CA : Red Hen Press, 2019.
Identifiers: LCCN 2018057504 | ISBN 9781597098991 (tradepaper)
Classification: LCC PS3610.I48 A6 2019 | DDC 811/.6—dc23
LC record available at https://lccn.loc.gov/2018057504

The National Endowment for the Arts, the Los Angeles County Arts Commission, the Ahmanson Foundation, the Dwight Stuart Youth Fund, the Max Factor Family Foundation, the Pasadena Tournament of Roses Foundation, the Pasadena Arts & Culture Commission and the City of Pasadena Cultural Affairs Division, the City of Los Angeles Department of Cultural Affairs, the Audrey & Sydney Irmas Charitable Foundation, the Kinder Morgan Foundation, the Meta & George Rosenberg Foundation, the Allergan Foundation, and the Riordan Foundation partially support Red Hen Press.

First Edition
Published by Red Hen Press
www.redhen.org

Acknowledgments

Thanks to Francisco Aragón and Letras Latinas, Rigoberto González, Sandra Cisneros, Dan Vera, Laurie Ann Guerrero, Douglas Kearney, and Victoria Chang for their belief in and attention to my voice.

Thank you to the Antioch University Los Angeles MFA in Creative Writing program for helping me see so many of the things my voice can do. Thank you to the Lucas Artists Residency Program and to my beloved Macondo Writers Workshops.

Thank you to DJ Alex Acosta, whose remixes I have listened to endlessly as I revised and revised these poems in search of a sound I wanted. And finally, to my friends and loved ones, including James and Randy and my circuit family, Howie, Mike, Abe, David, John, Jeff, Auston, and Taz, for helping me find that thing inside me that has allowed me to live the life I have always wanted to live.

for those of us who live for the nightlife

Contents

I

Woodsmoke   17

Whistling, or my beard is a feather into his mouth—.   19

On any given day, I am any other man
    who might forfeit his case to be good.   21

Next to his pillow, my first lover kept a cuete,
    & when we made love, sometimes my mouth pressed the hilt.   22

With a Hive of Bees under My Shirt   23

Love Poem for Two Homeboys Eating Chicanismo Like Ice   25

Sandblasters seem less a foe to my bones than the idea
    I will lose you because I have harmed you, Love.   26

There is nothing in me that
    can be another man's god—.   27

Baking chicken, I reach out to everything you
    & I silently love in the world.   28

II

Allegory of the Rattlesnake   35

Nocturne for Rattlesnakes and Lechuzas   37

Some nights, I just want to hold a man in my arms
    because this would make everything better in my life—.   41

Wood & Clouds Remix   42

The consequence of light—.   44

A pencil and a bowlful of pears.   45

Spit.   48

I'm afraid the house we're in will explode—.   49

What am I anymore if I'm not this?   54

Mesquites   57

III

Bone molt, or a man inside me believes an owl is growing inside.   63

Every minute I am making normal.   64

And what if I'm not more than any of this?   65

Quagmire   67

I could fall in love with another convict
     as easily as I read a sentence about shoes.   68

Armadillo   70

The Man in the Black Monte Carlo
     Came in Search of His Owls   73

Lechuza Sketch #11f   76

Lechuza Sketch #11g   77

Lechuza Sketch #11h   78

Lechuza Sketch #11i   79

Introduction

In the opening salvo, the speaker asks: "Have you never seen / love falter?" This is another way to consider: "Has love ever failed you?" Or even: "Have you ever failed at love?" However the question is angled, the witness becomes implicated and must reckon with a response. Or more pressingly, must reckon with memory. And that hurts even more because the fact of any uncoupling is that, inevitably, the heart(s) will shatter. Whatever thought comes next shapes the tone of the story of "that wide wingspan of lonely" that opens between former lovers. And it is on that newly formed space (because "the truth about lonely is it lasts") that the poet Joe Jiménez sings to the ache of longing and the pain of desire.

This journey, however, is not experienced in solitude: the aggrieved speaker pursues meaning and language in the desert's wondrous bestiary— the armadillo, the owl, the deer, the rattlesnake—each a spirit guide toward solace and reflection. The path to wildness, the search for the animal self, its brutal lessons in instinct and survival, is realized by invoking the wisdom of the queer borderlands as preached by Gloria Anzaldúa. Snake-bitten, the body must surrender to the realities of its vulnerability and its resilience. Snake-fanged, the mouth must contend with the violence of its venom and the fierce power of its poetry:

> Some nights I wake up
> inside
> my shadow, spit, and his whole breath a beast
> of unburdening, growing big.
>
> Some mornings my body marvels
> at its own hungers—

On the queer borderlands, Latino masculinity is complex. It is both tender and brutal. It might pine for a caress and then hide behind a shield. It is nurturing and threatening, love-starved and threatened, exquisite and exasperating. Take note of the seductive swagger of "a brown man with a machete & a necklace of hope." Jiménez certainly does, casting love and light upon the blessings of a wounded heart. If the stitching stings, restoration is happening; if yearning persists, there is life there still: "yes, I will keep my dark part breathing." But the most radical act is in making audible the silenced and censored narratives of queerness. The fear is no longer in being heard or discovered; the fight is against remaining unheard or invisible:

> In the world, some part of us is often
> unseen
> & not glorious.
> But what if it is?
>> Glorious. Seen.

Rattlesnake Allegory is a book about recharging the self after defeat, rising from the dust of rejection and dejection, resisting surrender. It takes plenty of strength and imagination, but those invigorating fuels are within reach. They have been written into our most inspiring books, they have been spoken by our myths, our landscapes, both magical and natural, and they have found their way into our body's rhythms—the breath and the heartbeat. "Listen to their milk," Jiménez directs, and learn, and grow, and heal. After the knowledge of the self as a flawed and spiritual being comes a dazzling rebirth.

—Rigoberto González

I

Woodsmoke

If I could kindle
a flame

out of water, it might
cost

the doors each of the locks,
which is all—
which is my plea
deal

with Godlessness.
Protection. Entryway, keys.

Once, I built
a fire out of a sofa—
because the world was cold,
& our house
gave no heat. But once

I fashioned a fast flame
from saliva,
I no longer feared

ending.
My life, like my father's—

that fencewire.
Mesh made of belt loops & charcoal,
coats, ten-gallon hats,
& gloves:

buckles from when we were boys:

Have you never seen
a man's whole body glow?

Have you never seen
love falter?

A falsetto, a faux note.
It is beautiful
to win, to bring out the best

in a man. Pero ten cuidado.
But be careful, I tell

these shadows—as they take small cottons
from my mouth

& listen to their milk.

& I tell them, You are glistening.
& I tell them, You walk too damn fast.

& Did I tell you about the hatchet
my father handed me:

hacking, combustion, whole slabs
of upholstery flaring
into ember, until ash?

It makes & unmakes me—
the smokes give
& forgive;

but ashes: Shit, those fuckers take
& they take.

Whistling, or my beard is a feather into his mouth—.

All day I can pretend I am not lonely.
All day I can fathom a catalog of gadgets
& twine, money
for milk, crumbs left by plum wine
& flint.

All day I can hope for a hoopla
I don't really want.

I don't want much, really.
Good air, today. Ants, maybe.
To watch, to carry away shit
I don't really, acutely need—to consume it.

A pile of dirt, maybe, which was bones
a century ago,
maybe a few blackbirds
& parts of a few trees—
long twigs, seed pods, root balls, & fronds—
so I can grow.
A mouthful of feather, of course, after,
like anything else, it has passed through
the body
& changed.

Yes, I still wonder if one day I will fly.

I want to say it is simple.
Like holding a man's hand.
Like placing my body inside his—

but I wouldn't call it that.
Or placing myself inside
one of his shadows, behind the myth
of his eyes, near the arc root of all gratitude,
what he loves
& thanks God for & is satisfied with . . .

Yes, wishes. Yeah, horses—

Because nothing is simple.
Because nothing really holds itself still—
unless it is Always, which is the swell inside
the ear bone of the back
that whistles every time we return
to places we loved . . .

Well, I miss my old life.
I miss it. Sometimes, I stand by my door, holding
my mouth in my hand,
wishing for someone to come by—

but it is not so simple as missing a man
I lost, or pressing my beard
into his mouth: *See how I've changed.*
Look at my back now, my arms.
Feathered—my eyes.
All of life is like this:
two skins or three—grazing—pressure, friction, horizon
lit & unlit & lit, again.

On any given day, I am any other man
who might forfeit his case to be good.

So I scatter myself like a storm—.

When I left the last man who didn't love me, a good woman advised me
about joining a cult: *Don't.*

The most beautiful thing a man's ever done for me is tear up his bed sheet.
So many perfect, off-white squares—cuadritos, into kites:

a blue ballpoint—firmesa, loveliness, but we are not the watchtowers,
& I forget where the peacock has run. O, you know the rest.

Featherness, that wide wingspan of lonely.

On good days, I long to lie back & whisper to mesquites.
Other days, I hold my breath so long I think I'll wake by the moon.
One day, soon—I long to hold an armadillo on my chest, listen to him
curl up & breathe.

What could I learn from his nine gray plates & claws?
More importantly, what might I do with my life after that?

Next to his pillow, my first lover kept a cuete,
& when we made love, sometimes my mouth pressed the hilt.

Openly—an asshole has often made me feel safe.
On occasion, a good man makes me feel frantic with red lights & Wild.
Typically, it's hard to tell if a man, deep in his fibers & bolts, is happy, is good.
But after loving, a man might tell you anything your body has jarred.
You've spilled him, perhaps. Split him open. Unshut him up.
Two hands that grow out of your tongue, grasping & gripping—
the whole inside him, slippery as ass,
slobbery melon, cantaloupe brawn, field's share of wet seed
& loose ties. Some days, I look out the window, hoping
to see a man who never loved me back, in his truck, smoothing by.
I wonder what asterisks he'd fill his hands with today.
I wonder what he'd think of my muscles or these poems.
Does he ever lie in bed full of nopales & fish hooks & bees?
Does he ever stand in front of a red lamp & remember my throat?
Less alone. Less silent. Less thirst-struck & slammed.
I admit it. I can't shout it. But I want it, & I am.

With a Hive of Bees under My Shirt

Like you, there are things I don't want anyone
to know.
Some days, I believe I walk the world
with a hive of bees
tucked beneath my shirt. As if only other bees
or people wearing harnesses sewn of drone wings
and honey might hear me.
Because I know the loneliness of a splinter
is loud.
The din of piquetes, also.
Because often, I want to pound nails into 2x5s
all day.
I want to sniff poems made only of mesquite
smoke and longing
on anyone who'll allow me.
I love a good pounding. But I also love the smell
of melancholy
in the fucked lines we pluck from our poems.
Over years, I have shared my bed with feuds—
most of them with myself.
My ganas are the size of an apiary, blindingly
full of buzz.
Because awe is a bolus weighted down by cinder
blocks and motherboards.
Mine? It sunk into the Gulf on a Wednesday.
When I was nine, I confessed to my priest
that I didn't love myself.
That's what it does to us: exasperation.
As a boy—I heard La Llorona whisper:
It is dangerous to remember.
As a man—La Llorona nuzzled my throat:
It is dangerous to want to forget.
Only dead birds and lechuzas with blindfolds

could see this.
Because my neurons are horse shrieks
and troughs full of howls.
I am a man who loves a good make-out session
with a ghost.
But then, I hate myself after the fact.
Always, it ends, because my mouth is so full
of questions,
I can barely use my tongue.
But why are splinters so lonely? And is my heart
really more than a museum?
How does the kneecap know to kiss the floor
when it prays?
What can I do with all these bees?
At its pinwheel pinnacle, the heartbag is shallow.
I don't always know how to save my own life.
I promise: I won't try and tell you
how to save yours.
Each Sunday, I plunged my thumbs into this hive
of bees.
Because the heart is riddled with seeds: the body's
own slow honeycomb.
When I was 35, I had to peel off my shirt.
The sun made a grandstand of the body's magic.
Last night, I tried to lure these bees
inside a box,
but sometimes, most times, they say they got shit
to do & they stay.

Love Poem for Two Homeboys
Eating Chicanismo Like Ice

Beneath us, the city said its name: Anthill
or Alien Metropolis—

the monolith of the heart is hard to fly with
unless two men, willingly, do the work of one,

but my mouth is not a moth, you said;
the night speech in my sleep sputtering: instead

we talked of birds who fed upon moths,
tall birds with ample, able wings—soft moths;

and this is urban talk: cinder blocks, de volada, mad
brains—drool, the tutelage of hogs, the vacant lots

of beds we left for the one we share:
thrillingly. And with you on my back I am a giant,

you, the brown hulk. Little airplane of the lungs
bending enough for fondness to gulp—.

Sandblasters seem less a foe to my bones than the idea
I will lose you because I have harmed you, Love.

I want you to forgive me | with that dim bud that is the rearside of love |
no processionals | no bouquets & red confetti for shit I've done—
teeth inside guilt sound off enough | I can turn off the TV to listen | I
can cast off my skin & be just autumn in your hand— | unpeeling guilt
leaves a fieldheap, & you, walking the monte of víboras & trees, cachetón.
| One day you'll bloom blame in a lake for some other man. | But I will
never forget your heart throbbing in my feet. | Ands, my buts, all the ifs
dissolve in huffing, or is it variation they're undergoing? | as for me |
I need the air | that is your beard, your thickset back | grunting & gasps |
But the part of you I will miss most is the seam I'll never fill | I'm under-
going guilt like an atom-smasher | & sandblasters seem less a foe
to my bones | than the idea I have lost you because I have harmed you, Love. |
So when I hold your sighs in my mouth just call it mesquite. | Just call it
lungs recalling water's crude sting | in whole gulps, in gobs, in
the foundplace you've brought me to. | Here's the burst trunk of penance,
here's the promise burying dogshit & bad teeth. | Uprootedness is only
a sin if we sniff the shit on God's knuckles. | Over there is the lake |
we'll never reach.

There is nothing in me that can be another man's god—.

All night I offer the dark fish
up for a beating.
       Fugitive fist, faux

tour guide
       of tight. Loneliness

& absolute zero choke back slobber,
           & I am too afraid to extol
aloneness
alone—.

So mirror, mirror—

       watch my knuckles teach self-pity
to clap.

Bent, all night, I can pinpoint
undialed skin,
       calamities I don't love—

typical tangle of taint

& toughness—
hair on my tongue will tell you my destiny.
       & Afterward, & afterward—

blindness glows far away.

Baking chicken, I reach out to everything you
& I silently love in the world.

Perhaps you are baking chicken
like I am baking chicken, with red potatoes
& quarter-moons of carrot, & at 425
in CorningWare, & with no bones, this means
we have thirty-five minutes. I cut the meat & lay down
the foil, & now, in these thirty-three minutes, you, like me,
might consider how your husband in the other room
is not thinking about you as he watches
Alex's good, pink tongue tattling its love for Piper,
& I am okay with this because
sometimes I need to be let alone,
let to take my thirty-one minutes & be.
Perhaps we are strangers. My husband
& my voice. You & me. Our lovers,
& everything you & I silently love in the world.
Perhaps we passed one another in the grocery aisle
this afternoon as I futzed through overripe
peaches, thumbing for good ones, as you held
up plastic Mexican blackberry crates, mesmerized
for that quasi-second by the clear perfection of black
that led, then, soon, marvelously, to the perfect
hue we call tartness. Perhaps your family,
like mine, will devour this sweetness—
never flinching to think what it took
to bring it to the mouth & its teeth.
Perhaps we are more than strangers,
but biology, like geographies,
has separated our souls since birth,
& so we have never met, except now,
except last winter when we both read
that same stunning poem about gorgeousness
& earth, how my heart said its name,
& yours, too, the real names they give themselves

when our hands are not all over them, picking them
apart or overgrowing them, & allowed,
aglow, they live, really—the hearts, the freed hands,
also, the whole body of the heart's brown eyes—
or perhaps we met when you were nine & I was seven,
& we both felt the same great bramble
of sadness when we discovered
where the red fern really grew. There are twenty-four
minutes left, & I have just enough time to open
myself & show you the redness, the fern that is mine;
you might do the same—& this is innocent;
no one should shout jealousy or rage.
Sometimes, I wonder how long that red fern
will grow inside of me: if it will go dormant
or lax or desiccate & grow trite & confused—
how can anyone ever know?
I admit it: I am thirty-nine & still afraid of not knowing everything
I'm supposed to. I feel nervous
when there are things a man is supposed to know
how to do, but I can't—.
I have eighteen minutes until the chicken is done,
& I know this: If you are like me,
perhaps there are things you've shown no one, tiny
pricks in your soul making honeycomb of the heart,
not even your wife or husband, whomever you love,
however you do it, not for any distrustfulness or deceit,

     but simply, simply because these are yours,
those sparrows & caracaras & soaring yellow cranes,
& also, & more importantly, just because you can,
because we are allowed to have some things alone,
just for you or for me—I am smiling,
& it will take twelve more minutes until my bird is cooked.
The McCormick in the air is enough

to upend the walls, floor planks, the bottle of white vinegar, & that water-
        stained sink I still need to clean
& can never clean right. I am preparing.
Cilantro rice. Pan-seared calabaza, too—
the green skin, oil, & seeds. I don't know
the ideas that stir in your body as the morning
shower's fingers contour your bones & cheeks,
& your chin like a gourd holds itself tightly, tightly,
in the wise hands of water, just before it releases—.
I think of lists. Perhaps you do, too.
I think of a man I once loved who disappeared,
of a book about people made of paper, which I loaned
to a friend, which she kept.
I think of my dog, who this time next year will be in my arms & dying,
        I think of summers at the shore
with heron & redfish keeping
the sound of bulrush that houses the ax
of my anxieties for what I've done & not done
with my life. In these moments, alone with my body,
I think of love, & are my exes happier
than I am? Was not choosing me the best thing?
When I was ten, I made a list of things
I wanted to accomplish by the time I reached thirty.
I wanted to be loved. I wanted tattoos like my dad
& thick arms like my mom's boyfriends, & a truck.
I wanted a house & a yard full of dogs.
Perhaps you also have a list, perhaps you also take count of your tallies,
        & does this make you
squeal—is it sadness, or zeal?
There are three minutes now remaining
until the chicken is baked, & I'll slide
the hot dish like a ship fleeing
hankering, fleeing dirges, exiled from sorrow,

& together, my family will eat,
with television blaring a talent show, & spoiled dogs,
back from the yard, gathered at our feet.
I will watch my husband
tell his kids from before me all about his day,
& I will feel joy that I can be here,
that I made this, that this is happening,
in part, because of me, because of people like us.
The clock has whittled itself down to a minute,
& so it is time for this moment I am sharing
with you to end, which means you & I—
we are no longer alone.

II

Allegory of the Rattlesnake

1

Under sun, in debris: a cascabel hums its whole nautilus
of fangdom and scales—a harmony.

But it came for us, we said. We heard, and we'd heard:
      They'll come for you. They lash out.
      Animus: pain :: And when it came—

As demon. As menace, as monolith, They as Goliath.

Everything we heard about rattlesnakes: cascabel
made of god but less godly
      than us—

2

Understand this: Anyone can suffer.

3

In my most Mexican self, I understand the sun built a fire, for he once was a god
who said: the body cannot be dispensed
      unless I allow it. So I kneel,
so I show the sun my slow throat and hope He can fathom me whole.
      I'd suckle obsidian for a chance. At wholeness.
      But ardor. But fear. Ayotzinapa. But prayer. Ferguson like Juarez.

4

Until I learn to unlove arrangements that make me.
Until I hold a man in my mouth like a mouse or a cricket, a white moth, a whole hare.

5

It is no surprise. We refute wholeness.
Of those we believe will do us harm:

He deserved it, we said.
Look at the shit he'd done.
What was she wearing?
Had it coming, so many of us agreed.

6

Because Fear is not an accident.

7

Ego hissing. Bravado that is blabbering. Cascabel's teat-pink suit, its fang wilt and coil.
Fiasco of scales and long rope.

Under debris, in sun: my body and his body your body her body their body—

on asphalt,
on hillsides,
in trash heaps,
in rivers,
in fires,
in a great desert—

As demon. As menace, as monolith, They as Goliath.

Anywhere in the world—anyone can suffer.

Nocturne for Rattlesnakes and Lechuzas

i.
Anzaldúa once admitted it took her forty years
"to enter into the serpent, to acknowledge I
have a body."
        I used to think I'd never hold forty
years
        in my mouth.

        She was cutting quelites with her
family. Wild Mexican greens. The ones that
had "outlived the deer's teeth."

        Fuck, she can write so beautifully.

        When I die, I want to also be buried
in deer's teeth. I want my mouth to fill
gently with sand and lechuzas.

        A few times I have thought of laying
my big body beside a deer—.

Near a road.
In a field made of huisache and moon—.

        To hold its long breath, to beg its hot
deerheart to beat slowly
        and only for me.

ii.
Tonight, I near 40: I trace an owl on a pad,
watch a television show where people make
beautiful things
      out of organza and seams.

The owl steadies my hand:
      wing coverts, tarsus, face-disc—
      scapulars and steam.
      My wrist believes it is young.
      Control comforts a heartspan,
where it rests.
      Alula, it seems—

but I also want to make beautiful things—.
      Sometimes, I want others to see me
as beautiful, too.
      Not rough, not voracious.
      Not ever wielding the machete of my
body, splitting anyone in two.

      But I don't want to have to lose
the brownness I'm in to obtain it—
beauty,
gentleness, flight—.

      My body is full of tunnels.
Hollowness, but not like a bird's.

I'm ashamed for fearing heights,
      so I'd make a really fucked-up bird.

Sometimes, I think not wanting to look out the window of a high-rise makes me less of a man.

Sometimes, I fear the dim, firm husk that grows over me makes me more of one.

iii.
In the anecdote Anzaldúa shares, she is
snake-bitten, she can feel venom in her
body, and she buries the rattlesnake that
bites her

      "between the rows of cotton."
She says this on page 48.

She says the earth is a coiled serpent.

And she is immune.
           Often, I wish I, too, could
bury the rattlesnake. Maybe digging
a hole is where my beauty will be found.

But I haven't been in a cotton field in a good
grip of years.

But sometimes, I simply want the snake
to enter me, to coil inside me

      and stay.

      Most times, I just wish I could spend
all night digging holes in a field
of huisache
and deer hearts and moon—
      as if anyone could still be immune.

**Some nights, I just want to hold a man in my arms
because this would make everything better in my life—.**

a comfort I frame—biceps and all
of my Mexican tattoos, my bulldog chest, and stuttering lung,
whispers that come only from another man's scalp
when the whole world inside him is a fingernail
or quiet like a small bucket of snails.
Even when I'm a remolino,
more so, then, especially, I wish my kiss tenderness,
enough to make a man's heart burst
into a thousand desert owls—wingbeat,
featherness, beak prod, and screech.
Last week, I was a pendulum in a fantasy—versatile,
swinging back, forth, into, deeply.
Being entered is when I know I am human.
Being entered is when I know I'm a part of something bigger.
Again. Equilibrium.
Evenness. And here it is: I've come here to love
breath in my bones when skin falls off the world.
and who doesn't carry some sort of trap on his knuckles?
The moment inside the body
when joy is not born as much as it is made out of anything
the rest of the world doesn't want.

Wood & Clouds Remix

1. Indeed, holding a man is formless.
2. A body deprived will stutter its mass, a field test in slobber.
3. A man is a body; a man is also a cloud & a moment, a trajectory, an idea.
4. Nothing murmurs forever: not a thing so slurred will last.
5. & Forever exists to molecules, not only for the nextness of the heart.
6. Forever as all the throat can cite when it's gagging.

1. Though I haven't slept inside a mouth made of wind.
2. Though formlessness is nonetheless a form.
3. Though I haven't slathered my torso & thighs in patience procured via bone-work with deer & the slow elk of waiting.
4. Though the heart is also a bone & the bone is also a breath.
5. Though air busies its lungs with asterisks & endnotes for how to etch a heart's red belly with echo & good moan.
6. Though man's slobbery body, his eye-heart & belly's slurred bent hands.
7. Though imprint, though memory.
8. Though forever & ever amen.

~

1. When I die, I want it to be heavenly.
2. When I die, I want no one to gag.
3. When I die, I hope worms that devour me
   are gods, the wood louse, the flies' teeth, also.
4. I think anything can be a God.
5. I think God loves every shit-thing & beauty.
6. I think molecules can etch anything they hold
   with nextness & waiting.

~

1. But deer hearts & elk pelts stretching over my
   loneliness.
2. Take a moan by the hand, see what good it does.
3. So give me a coffin made of buck hearts
   & wood,
4. Each nail a stuttering test of two odd clouds.
5. I pray beetles & flies take every part of me, turn
   me to something better than God,
6. Make something new.

The consequence of light—.

I remember the first time I took off another man's shirt.
I folded it. After I folded mine—
& I made neat little squares & placed the squares on the bed.
Light fell on his neck,
his quagmired chest—callus, announcement, watchtowers
spelling things he hadn't had—.
I've found the most harmful part
inside us is blunt disregard juxtaposing the body's bidding, the need.
Gray ink & seams, echoes made of keeping things hidden.
Your hands are very rough, he said.
I was looking for a place for my life to happen.
But thumbs in my mouth quivered, two jars holding back flames.
My tongue is the starting point—
built into the throat is the idea that our bodies are made of cairns.
I understand where I will end up—
& I can't spend my life trying to tell you why I am good.

A pencil and a bowlful of pears.

Often, I wish I'd been with more men.
Sadly, but sadly, a man's body
is the slingshot I feared.
Simple impossible tenderness.
Dreamscapes and butterscotch, Listerine
and landmines.
I can't tell you one kind of madman
from a handful of teeth.
I can't tell sadness from a pencil
and a bowlful of pears.

But I can tell you my body is a nest braided
from hush,
a catapult of upthrown stones.

Breath is more bitter when it empties
its hands
into cuffs,

and the world may have built us from ribs,
or from mud.
I don't care. I don't.

In the rucksack of hog belly and gloves, I
still ask God,
Why am I not quelled enough
by shadows that sweat?
How might I undo this slack?
Or widen my throatbone so I swallow
shit best?

The answer
is a shadow that kisses its own fists, a tooth
willing to eat any darkness;

the answer
is who hasn't ever wanted to unbitter
his body?

All night I might fathom taking back
something precious
that somehow,
long ago, or not so long, I don't know,
ripped off,
yanked from bone,
sloughed off like a husk.

The truth about loneliness is it's lonely.

The truth about lonely is it lasts.

For whole moments, life spans,
less so.

But to clutch and to glow, to hatch,
to show . . .

Isn't that the point of the point we are
making with breath?

Once in a coffee shop,
I watched
a man sketch a handful of pears.

So it might last, I wanted to place
my parts
in his bowl—

palms or mouth or asshole.
O, does it matter?
None of it sits well when I say it
out loud.

These words as strangers I can't make
myself finish off and eat.

Spit.

Some nights, the wrong thing inside us is joy.
& how I wish every other idle plume
to cast away so that all I know, then, is joy—
all I have.

Perhaps this edge of the fingernail is living.
Perhaps the secret to loving oneself is all
in the spit.
What it's about—
to remind the throat it escaped
the pit full of belly . . .
the edict only to be breath or bone . . .
Nothing more—

but my life is more than halfway over, & again
I tell the mouth as it kneels:

We do this for bodies made now only of breath.
We do this in memory of grief.

I'm afraid the house we're in will explode—.

the hardest part about loneliness | is not when he bludgeons your heart |
with a toothpick | or when he slides | the exit ticket under the door |
like a small gray tooth, | but it's difficult I can tell you | bc I've done it
twice before: when you love him | & he loves you, he says, | but the two
worlds you grew in are Pluto & Mars, | if he even considers Pluto
a world | & doesn't debate it when you say, It is— | that I exist, |
in no less a world than a world equal to his | | |

—but maybe he never considered people like us | existed | & worked
hard, set goals, had ethic, | got hungry, | rarely were fed enough, | or held
by their mothers | or read to, | told: You will be something great, boy,
The world is all yours, | Do something big & important with your life. |
Did something obscure his view? | a rocket ship careening |
across pupils? a belt made of asteroids | making it too hard for eyes
to breathe? | maybe just a satellite | flying in front of the whole wide
heart? | | |

I don't know how else to say it. | I don't think a metaphor would be apt,
| no vehicle | to split open the hum: but the body will not always tell
how it connects to what it wants or how. | so I don't know I believe this,
even when I say it twelve times a day, | even when I write it on the skin of my
lung's hand | but I tell him the day our food stamps arrived— | we
called it "Mother's Day" & rejoiced & ate whole bags of chips & bananas,
| weenies & drank soda & purple Kool-Aid all at once, | but he chuckles,
| bc why on earth would anyone feel joy on a day like that? |
shame, that's what he'd feel. | | | perhaps like me, you fell in love |
before they hurt us with syllables & ideas about food | & electric bills
& sounds like gritos & want, | not knowing it would matter
that they be able to grasp | our lack | like an apple, | how it means
to know absence | like need | like the pit of some gnawed plum, | a bite
made of kindness. | a gulp of welfare & impossible sums. | | |

& I still fear having nothing. | do you? still petrify | at having to spend the last modest sum | I've saved—to eat that last egg. | I want to save everything, | bc some bad unforeseen shit is likely to occur at some point in my life. | you know how this works, | after all, you heard lessons in your mom's salt | when she showered | or sobbed in the backyard alone, | a dark tree, & no moon, holding a bill, | wanting no one | in that house to hear. | how then | would you deal? | | |

beneath your manbody he may seem frail | a small hungry cub or a big-
eyed seal, | mouth opened wide | or begging for it, maybe it's the old
odd fuse, | you are dangerous & I am dangerous | O, yes, | O, yes.
foreskin & brown skin, peligro & Mexican teeth, | that being near your
thickness, | succumbing to your body with its darknesses, | & thick
myths, | its bootleg tattoos & sacred hearts are what buzzes him, | drives |
him wild, | exhorts his controls: | how they flung to him with ropes
or came hooked | with his birth, | how they connect & unravel & bind, |
bc maybe this is how | he loves me & is the big hero, loves himself, |
saving me | somehow from catastrophes | he doesn't know what my body
can really survive, | I don't know, I don't know a goddamn thing
about loving | a rich man when we've been poor | all our lives, | everyone
had more, we were always running out, | it's in the land in our bones, |
scribbled on our necks like a bad ex's name, you can't ever let go, |
except that it feels good in my heart | & all around my fat ass & inside
each morning | when I pull him around my breath | & make him say
who I am, not my name, | but that surrender of his own vein-ribbed
echoes when I'm done. | my poor heart is very hot, | my poor heart
is tired of what it's not, | I used to believe I could change the world, |
I used to believe I was special. | some days I'm afraid the house we've
built will explode, | some days | I need more than this body I'm in | to feel
this is home | | |

What am I anymore if I'm not this?

The river is only full of gar

       as long as I am afraid.
In quicksilver fins, gar may carry
alligator, but their scales are gorgeous

because they are more than human,
and less than.

But the sun is rising yesterday. But wind
is heavier

     than dust.

Away is where they say promises show up
when you carve
open fruit to find no seeds.

Me? I can cut shit open with my teeth.

Juices sluice knuckle, beard unfurls
my jaw,
& all my life I've wanted

only to be good.

At the moment I fear is the only reason
I don't change.

∾

Some nights I wake up
inside
my shadow:

                spit, and his whole breath
a beast
of unburdening,
growing big.

Some mornings my body marvels
at its own hungers—

a hankering
        to swim beside gar,

floating among their fat upcast shafts,
spooning
their wide, tube-long skins, .
careening
silver-scaled girths, garbodies
to my throatbone,

                & black chin
begging them
to listen, begging
them to let my lips scrape
the long veinthrob
& flex.

∾

In every whisper there is hunger
& shadows.
In every hunger there is a river.
In every deep unseen there is terror
and there is joy.

∾

So if I let my whispers open their throats,
what other magic is there?

Peligro. Hunger, ganas—
                every river has a bottom.
So if you know hunger like this. Toma.
Take one
of my teeth,
press it

        to a shadow. Then, eat.

Mesquites

In a field a plethora of mesquites grew.
Rampantly, some of them unruly. Wildness
and fending off shames. Shames? you may ask.
For being bent, for shaping in unnatural ways.
It was said. And so it was—.
But magic, for none of these were trees
in the sense that trees should take root
and not tremble or growl or know Love
for one other. Water and wind. Earth,
Light. Saplings, thus groves. And some spread
their seedpods for the sole sake of giving them
up or taking another's seed. And pleasure
and wildness—. Earth and Light.
And this was the world.

Then. Something emerged
among the mesquites. And overcome,
unprepped, how the mesquites suffered—.
Over time, seed pods grew strange, dire.
The field soon became a field.
People witnessed. Mesquites began
gradually, forthwith, to die off—.
So many of them. No one
could halt that suffering, though so many tried.
And distance and Grief—.
And heavy murk where once fullness
and Joy, and Wonder. A sad hymn
of sinews: mottled shadows, emptiness—.
For years, the hymn hummed.
Harrowed, the field knew somberness
as if it were wind and Light,
the field knew erosion and understood
what loss uttered to its bones: the spirits

of every bird and the tall yellow grasses,
the souls of all the mosses
and the armadillos
digging grubs from the most tender soils,
the little deer
who relied on the mesquites
for shade, the coyotes who satisfied hungers
with the pods—. For many years, then: loss,
affliction, tribulation, woe.

　　　　In time, in time, the mesquites
would return to the field. Newer ones,
and yes, some of the original ones, too,
older, unbroken. Often forgotten,
the surviving mesquites stood tall,
while the new ones easily fed on the field,
the nourishment of those mesquites
who had come before and given of themselves
to the soils on which we all stand.
And this newness was newness, too brash
and swaggering—. Sometimes, solipsism
and disregard—. But I can tell you
there are minutes, whole afternoons, full
seasons where a mesquite will feel unpresence—
the knot in its deepest wood or a hiccup in the root
span, and how it knows, for how can its body
not know that someone was once there?
An emptiness of spirit—a little voice
carried on the soft back of wind.
I tell you it happens, the mesquite
compelled to feel an aloneness only known
by mesquites of this field, for someone

should be here beside him, but isn't—.
And you might call this outlandish,
or you might comprehend this suffering,
the idea of all mesquites carrying this epoch—
and why? and how? and who? and does it ever
go away?

      In a field a plethora of mesquites grows.
Rampantly, and some of them unruly. Wildness
and fending off shames. Shames? you may ask.
For being bent, for shaping in unnatural ways,
it was said. But magic. But water and wind.
Earth, Light. Saplings and seedpods,
whole groves.

III

Bone molt, or a man inside me believes an owl is growing inside.

1. Today, I want something more than an old whisper
   to live in.
2. Some hours I am a memory of a boy and a kite
   and a paño and a bike,
3. that spinning planet someone else gave us.
4. Some mornings, I put my face in a sink, wishing to see
   an armadillo.
5. I am no longer young. I don't usually fixate
   on beautiful.
6. A man inside me believes an owl is growing inside.
7. Every splinter of his joints, or hers, offering something
   no one else in the world could give.
8. Or ever has.
9. What can we call this?
10. All I hear is the moon: all her parts, becoming one.
11. Bone molt and plumules, vane & shaft, barbs.
12. Munificence of muscle, spectacle of unclaimed breath?
13. A part of it all, perhaps. Largesse.
14. Flesh splits like dawn, my big legs spread for nopales
    and mesquites, wind.
15. Dusting of echoes, dusting of seed.
16. Two parts: quantum of old life, universe of the new.
17. I will always be one to fathom a past where I don't belong.
18. I will always be one to wish for things I know aren't
    mine.
19. Yes, I am leaving. Yes, the grief-egg of my heart.
20. This is my grunting. Echo or moan?
21. A man echoes more when a part of him is gone.

Every minute I am making normal.

Every minute I am making normal. | unmaking this shit-day or that one.
| take any part of my boy | bones, everything I've eaten, but |
the kinds of men I've had, | now that yields some down-ass spiels about
my body. | | now, how I made them | mine, | shit, that's the real
story of my brown. | swallowed like pills, | ground whole by ridgy junk
molars. | jaw-nibbled mote by mote or quick-chewed | in giant, girthy
chunks | & bit, sopped crumbs: | doing bad shit just means the good shit
wasn't good enough to choose. | last week I shipped a sketch | of my old
life, | & in my lover's mouth | teeth clicked or tongue. | teeth
& red-throat | rage: was it really that bad? | a too-green gourd split
open like a boy's dark part, | & two opossums fighting over the seedy
heart. | | the sweetest part of not having is coveting, | then getting. |
even sweeter: being coveted—jittering black weeds all over my chin
& hawknose, my floor-sore knees. | | normal is looking | the years
in the eye & saying, Now what? | | does the floor need to be swept
before I kneel again? | whose turn is it to wash | the mugs & forks?
where the hell did you put my good comb? | | right now the mop
calling my name can be ignored, | a brown man with a mop might be
a potent thing. | but a brown man with a machete & a necklace of hope;
now that's some dangerous shit. | | fill a bucket of fabulous suds |
if I am not making normal with every strange tweak, | whose life am I
unmaking? | whose man am I undoing? | by making my life teem | |
yes, I will keep wielding this machete & necklace of seeds | yes, I will
keep my dark part breathing.

And what if I'm not more than any of this?

Once, I saw a great gar tear apart a gull.
Yes, my abuelo bottled his fat knuckles
about my neck,
my boythin chin—
      said, "Look."

The sound Sun makes when it rises can be heard
if I listen with brown skin I no longer speak,
which is a flare gun,

      a codex spared by God.

After, the gull wing floated in the dark river.
A little sailboat.

      A little smoke.
      A sigh doped-up with patience, dropped
from the sky.

All day, I can reach for that gull.
All year. It won't mean
I want to leave the river behind.

It won't mean I can't kneel for fruits that kiss earth.
Offer them to satisfy order, to defy.

Most days, I don't mind
laying my blown boybones down in the mud
on the shore
near the sedge
      under sun.

I only hope I keep enough good teeth.
I just hope someone, somewhere
remembers
shadows also deserve to eat.

Quagmire

There is a quandary. A mare's nest inside me, a quagmire of atoms
and fixations. To be solved, or stalled,
      or turned to red slough, who can say?
and is it even there? If I summon its namesake, if I point and run
      my nose through dark twigs in its hair?

In the distance, the ripped bale, the hay-strewn field. Cattle
      egrets, the wedding sun.
Yesterday, I came to this field thinking it might fix me; in the box
      of my truckbed,
I crossed my arms, lay down, stared at red centaurs in clouds.
I wanted to be one: a centaur. But wind had to tell me I don't come
      from satyrs or centaurs but owls.
In this case, I have forgotten when trespassing is wrong.
Before night, I built a wreath of coal and of hair, of logs, and of hay,
      unbridled, left to flow. I made fire.

I was lonely. I asked God for birds, but He gave me a wheelbarrow
of armadillo and horse bones, corn husk and mud.
      and what is it holding me back?
Can I call it gloom? a doom-stop of clocks and fence posts,
      fat cables, leather bits?

All day I will sit on my tailgate, the field and the fire-wreath
      trying to keep inside me.
In this case, I can no longer bolster any hoax with tenderness.
In this case, I can no longer pretend I do not love the field, maybe more
      even than I love myself.
Hands burned, my boots sinking in mud, I say my mother was wrong,
because I can't find the wealth she said I would find in suffering.
      No, when does aguanto bloom?

**I could fall in love with another convict
as easily as I read a sentence about shoes.**

Could wrap him in nestling built of subpoenas,
old electric cords,
& hush

    —all the bad things my brownness can do.

In a poem, once, I described my heart as a gray mollusk—

squeezing.

Whole years in my life I have wanted just to hold
a man's bad bone.

Distant friction

    —muffled Gulf sigh, owl screech, lie.

As if sorrow might be scraped away with teeth,

drawn from a body,
spit out,

    —consumed.

As if love could be this compact:

taking another's ache between molars, or two
of your sighs,

    —doing with it.

A man I once loved tried to die right in front of me.
                Ache holds some of us together—

& I'd been taking that away.
                    Most of that night I held him

until birds in his groans could no longer strain
from the warmth—

I will remember the dim hum of his breach—

eaten now by slow moths in my heart,

the great owl
that slakes its own calls in the fields of bulrush
& smutgrass
growing

stronger
        —inside my bones.

Armadillo

A boy once snatched a Polaroid. Armadillo snapshot.
Clicked near a Diamond Shamrock on a quick trip
to the little town where the boy was born,
just after his father grabbed his littleboy dick,
put it to a Gatorade bottle's glass rim, told him, "Piss, boy."
In a sock drawer, the boy stashed the armadillo.
Beneath jockstraps & muscle cars, beneath a tin cup
of nickels & welts, the armadillo lived,
because sometimes the world refuses to stop for us,
& I wish I could hold your hand as I tell you it is okay
to feel afraid when we take things we're not supposed to
have—hoard them, hide them, make believe they're not ours.
Did you know the most dangerous part of happiness
is knowing those ideas we keep don't own bodies?
They don't. No heartbeat, no self, no right to live their lives.

So the little gray beast
made of lightbox, made of pins,
made of aguanto,

built of skin.
It dug. & All night, & for years after that:
A dirt hole.
Snarl of dens. Gnarly vault.
Like the one growing beneath the boy's spine—
not idle,
but dark.
But thudding. But deep.
Because the point of horn-covered bone is not plating:
but love for one's body,
but fear. Because smallness
made of wonder. Because joy.

In bed, the Monte Carlo sped. The boy steadied his body,
mouth clamping down. In the back, he'd drained, straining
the cap tight, tossing his piss out the window toward
a field near the shoulder away from the rough road.
Sometimes the world goes by so fast; rows of cotton,
years & wishes & grunts. The boy wiped his hand;
the father was the father; the bottle spun the road. Slash
of golden glint, halo of piss. But wind stomachs its own ache
& sometimes every winged thing you want to say won't
remember its own name. In his room, the boy took
the little armadillo from its box, beneath jocks & muscle car
mags. Lay with it on the bed. Mouth opened its long watch.
He held the little armadillo to bones in his chest.
Again, again. Lungs promised muscles not to worry, just live.

The Man in the Black Monte Carlo
Came in Search of His Owls

Owl
In el monte, a long-rooted wind slid into an owl. The owl
perched in a tree. The tree perched inside the owl. Owl
beak, talons. Root snarl, cypress. Cicadas shriek: each
time wind came through its teeth, bark slurred.

Grunts
Cicada-clad oaks grunt their guilts—beckon wind, summon
owls. Leaves spill ovals & swoop. Sweeping cypress
watching, knowing every spliced envy, open like a hog
steaming over coals, half gone. In breeze, tree muscles
clap odes.

Monte Carlo
Trees muscle an ode to a man I never became. Blunt-jaw,
scab-jowl, driving a Monte Carlo. Black tar car. Knuckles
& biceps bulge, fist built & thick. The world inside owls
watching him nail tripe to trees. As trophies. He made my
father proud. & My mother, bendita, sang songs to her
friends about all the shiny shit he'd done.

el Monte
Shit I could never do will slide across an old caliche road.
There's a map somewhere to be found. There's a lesson to
be learned in crushed shell, that white dust. But there is my
mother & there is his father, & there we are, eating cabrito,
sitting on smashed logs, stroking our lungs.

Man
Our lungs will bleat their Unwillingness, but isn't
Unwillingness also a place for the sloppy bud of a body to
groom? Toe arch, heart bulkier. & What of my heart's odd
couplings—inkslung rings, skewed brown girth—left inside
of itself, which were my father's wishes for me? which
were ways I smeared? Trees moan. Still a long way to walk.

Somewhere, there is a horse.
A long walk to stillness, & sometimes, I am the man who
cannot bear to hear it—the two-ton heartbeat of the hoof.
But if I squat beneath a bald limb near a dark river,
contemplating the man I don't become—his square bare
feet, hand-heft made thick by mounds & forgiving—*No
llores, chiquito. Don't cry, little one—forgiveness is a trick
thirsty boys can show you to turn.* Footsteps of rabbits,
dark jowls of stags—don't you hear it, too?

Physiologies
& Don't you hear the Wind: a curdle of air, gale, breeze . . .
as in "the trees were swaying in wind." . . . as in "the owl
molts in the bone's slow winds."

Owl: the hooked beak, pinpoint hearing, nightbird, raptor . . .
as in "the owl turned to look at the man hammering
stag guts into trees."

Tree: root gnarl, x, y.

Proximities

x & y, I forget the equation, but in the presence of absence,
I am fulfilling my skin—is bandaging ache using lining
from animal yowls any real fix? To repair urge is a refusal
to settle in, shut the mouth's eyes: deploy stare into
sunlight, javelina tusk pressed against Patience's scalp.
Mustered up, shredded strength still is strength.

Tendencies

Strength will shred my stillness with Wind's teeth. Roots,
shrieks. Offals & falling. On its echo, the blunt heart's
wide gape. An owl's jagged qualms cough inside me:
in a mirror, all I see smokes—*understand that a piece exists
for having been broken.* Whole pedasote or jagged
pedacito—which grunts more hope?

Lechuza Sketch #11f

For days, I have been asking
if I have it.

I can't tell you if my bones are enemies
or not.

Sometimes the body changes so much
it's impossible

to know all its turns & its sums.

Ochre patches, hair rings—quasi-plumes
loom near lungs, hanging

—a sick moss.

& What did I do to merit this heinous tangle
of hollow & moan?

All night, I will stand at the end of this pier.

I hold the dark sky with thumbs
                    in my mouth—

a white fire trembles.

Lechuza Sketch #11g

By hollowness, I mean bones, by bones
I mean echo.

       Tough-drawn, the heartclaw
shuts its red eye.

High clouds,
or a soft forestry of gray trees:

       the Gulf asks what I am.

but don't all things make their own
beginnings?

& Won't all things come to an end?

Some nights I hear a thousand horses
speaking at once—

two or five or sixteen versions standing
on a yellow cliff
is a real test of standing at all.

but sometimes muscles are not muscles;

& Sometimes the clavicle is just a cough.

A little flickering in the bird-chest.

White flower, an unreachable wait.

Lechuza Sketch #11h

Waves move in with their appetites.

An uncompromising warmth
has come.

              My shape is breaking
the wish, still.

Each night, the spine calls—
& I am whistling,

trying to answer back.

Sea hiss & salt: false eyes

glint. I want to cast my old self
out like a net, aside.

It isn't clear how I hear the sturdy bone
of that storm.

In some of us there is a sharp petal,
a grunt—

        an unborn lightning.

Lechuza Sketch #11i

All my life I will stand on the dark pier.

The wing will shiver & quake.

Gulls leave me behind.

Yes, I know there is not one saved
place for every live thing

in the world.

      Yes, I know.
A storm in the Gulf

in my body: the lovesong of echoes
& cliffs.

Over time, my face will clack, it will
croak.

This body will crash into light.

Fickle memory. Sickle salt.

Some hours, I don't know
if I am becoming something better.

In the world, some part of us is often
unseen
& not glorious.

But what if we are?
      Glorious. Seen.

Biographical Note

Joe Jiménez is the author of the poetry collection *The Possibilities of Mud* and the young adult novel *Bloodline*. Jiménez is the recipient of the 2016 Letras Latinas/Red Hen Press Poetry Prize. His poems have appeared on the PBS NewsHour and Lambda Literary sites. Jiménez was recently awarded a Lucas Artists Literary Artists Fellowship from 2017 to 2020. He lives in San Antonio, Texas, and is a member of the Macondo Writers Workshops. For more information, visit joejimenez.net.